Angela Knapper

FRIENDS

FOREVER

Simply Black and White

To my husband Sean who has always

believed in me and pushed me to be as

great as he thinks I am, and my two closest

friends Ms. Yvette and Sandy who have

always believed in me.

Contents

Chapter One

"She's been in her room for two days. She won't eat, she hasn't slept and she only leaves her room to go to the bathroom. Tom I'm worried about her."

"Pam, she just lost her best friend. She's hurting, she just needs time," Tom told his wife. "She'll come around."

"I know, I know. I just hate seeing her like this," Pam said almost in tears. "She won't talk to anyone, not Tony or even Jeremy."

"Give her time; she'll talk when she's ready."

"I think I'll bring her something to eat," Pam told her husband.

As Pam walked up the stairs, she passed pictures of her daughter as she had grown up. She wondered what she could possibly say to make Rose feel better. Pam got to her daughter's door, knocked, and waited for an answer.

"Who is it?" a small, weak voice asked.

"It's me; I have something for you to eat. Can I come in?" Pam asked as the door opened.

"I'm not hungry, Mom," said a girl of about 18, with brown curly hair and green eyes which were all red and swollen. You could tell she'd been crying for some time. She walked over to her bed and collapsed onto it.

Pam walked in and saw the floor littered with tissues. She also saw photo albums and pictures all over the place.

"Rose, you've got to eat something. This

isn't what Angie would want you to do."

Pam set the tray of food on the desk and picked up the closest picture. The photo showed two girls with ear-to-ear grins. The one on the right was Rose; the other was a bit taller, with blonde hair and bright blue eyes that smiled. At the sight of this, tears started to well up in Pam's eyes, after all she thought of Angie as her daughter too.

"I know. I just..." Tears filled up in Rose's eyes as she fell silent.

"You just what?"

"I just miss her so much!"

"I know, I know, but you need to eat, sleep, and get out. Jeremy and Tony have called at least fifty times in the last two days."

"Jeremy? How's he doing?"

"About as bad as you, I guess. He really

wants to talk and see you. Maybe you should give him a call. It might help to talk to someone who's going through the same thing," Pam suggested.

"I don't think I'm ready to talk to him yet," she admitted, looking down at what appeared to be a very long letter.

"What's that?" asked Pam following Rose's gaze.

"This? Well, Mrs. Thompson gave it to me. She said Angie wrote it and that she was to give it to me after Angie..." Rose couldn't even finish she was crying so hard.

"Have you read it yet?" Pam asked.

"I can't get past the first sentence."

"Why not?" Pam was shocked at this. "What does it say?"

"Rose, I love you!" Rose's voice was barely a

whisper.

Pam ran over and put her arms around her daughter. No words of comfort came to her. So she sat there, holding Rose and said nothing. She didn't have to; it was enough that she was there.

After about fifteen minutes, Pam asked, "Have you thought about what you're going to say at the funeral?"

"No! I haven't even thought about it; I don't want to."

"Well you better start thinking. The funeral is in two days." Pam gave her daughter a final hug and left the room.

Rose watched her mother leave. She sat there for along time just staring at the closed door.

"How can they possible expect me to give a speech when I can't even stop crying? I can't even begin to think of anything to say. Angie was my best friend; I should have tons of things to say about her. Why can't I think of one solitary thing?" Rose asked herself out loud.

Rose walked over to her desk and glanced at the food her mother had brought up to her. She hadn't realized how hungry she was. She took the sandwich and started to eat. Then she walked back to her bed and picked up the letter Angie had written and lay down. She was going to read this letter even if it took all night.

Chapter Two

Rose, I love you! You have been my best friend forever and you always will be. We've been through so much together. My mom use to say if you're looking for Angie you'll find Rose and vice versa. We were inseparable. I never wanted to do anything unless you could do it too, and if you couldn't then I wasn't going to. But we both knew that could never always happen or neither of us would have had much of a life. We've stuck together through thick and thin, good times, bad times and really bad times. You've always been there for me no matter what I was going through. I only hope that I was always there for you when you needed me.

Do you remember when we first met? I remember it like it was yesterday. It was the first day of kindergarten for us. I was so nervous that no one was going to like me. When I walked into the classroom, there you were. The teacher sat us next to each other and once we got over our shyness that was it, we were friends for life.

I'll never forget our first sleepover. You were so scared of my brothers and didn't want to stay so we had to bring you home at like twelve o'clock at night. So the next time I slept at your house and things went much better. And up until junior high we had done everything together and had always been in the same classes.

Chapter Three

Junior high is where the fun really started. We were so worried that we wouldn't be in any of the same classes as this is when we started changing class rooms instead of staying in just one all day. It would kill us if we had to be separated.

"Rose, what if you aren't in any of my classes? I'll just die! What if I don't know anyone?" Angie asked her best friend just before they looked at their schedules for school.

"Angie, you'll be fine. You'll know tons of people. Everyone who meets you loves you. You're the most popular person I know. Plus we can still do everything together," Rose reassured her friend. "It will only be while we're in school. You act like we'll never see each other if we aren't in the same classes."

We didn't have to worry about that though, did we? We ended up in all the same classes except for one or two. And that was the way it usually was.

Do you remember the time when we were in sixth grade and we wanted to go camping but couldn't talk anyone into taking us? So we decided to set up camp (or try to) in my backyard.

"Would you girls like some help? I don't think you'll be able to do it by yourselves," came a man's voice from inside the house.

"No thanks Dad, we got it," Angie yelled back to her father.

From in the house Mr. and Mrs. Thompson watched the two girls try to set up the tent. The two of them got a good laugh watching. Then again they usually did when the girls were together. Outside the two girls were trying with all their might to get the tent set up by themselves.

"No, no, that pole goes over here," Angie instructed.

"No it doesn't. It goes here where I had it," Rose protested.

"Are you sure?" Angie asked looking around. "I don't think all the pieces are here."

"They have to be!" Rose said starting to get very frustrated.

About an hour later the girls, somewhat, had the tent set up. So they got inside to start their camping trip. About ten minutes later, Mr. and Mrs. Thompson heard screams coming from the backyard. They ran out back to see what had happened. When they got to the back door they didn't have to ask. They just stood at the door and laughed.

In the place where the tent had been now

lay a pile of blue with two big humps in the middle. After the girls had gotten into the tent it had fallen apart. The girls didn't bother to try to fix it. They just got their things and went up to Angie's room and had their camp out there.

Chapter Four

Or how about the time we went to Michigan for my cousin's graduation? I had to beg my mom and dad to let you come with us. Then you had to do the same with your parents. Remember? We told our parents that you had to go so that I wouldn't be bored and feel left out. And that we never got to go away together. We couldn't believe it when they said yes. It was all we talked about till we left. We had so much fun. The trip there was a blast.

"We get the back!" Angie yelled to her

brother Dan.

"I don't care! I'm sitting in front," he yelled back. Dan was tall and thin with blue eyes and dirty blonde hair.

"No you're not!" protested Angie's other brother Steve, who was even taller then Dan and much heavier, with dark eyes and brown hair. "I am!"

It was about three in the afternoon on a Wednesday early in June. The Thompson family was packing up the van getting ready to go to Michigan. Mr. Thompson was driving; Steve was in the passenger seat, Dan and Mrs. Thompson were in the second seat and Angie and Rose were in the third. The two girls sat in the back and talked the entire way. There wasn't a moment of silence the whole way there. Finally, to the relief of everyone, they arrived.

"Everybody out," Mr. Thompson said after the car was parked.

"Hi! It's about time guys got here," came Angie's aunt's voice. "How was the drive?"

"Way too long and very annoying!" Dan

answered, shooting the two girls a peeved look.

"Yeah and I'm not looking forward to the ride home either," Steve added.

They got their things and went into the house. Angie introduced Rose to everyone, even though mostly everyone knew her and considered her part of the family. The rest of the night was pretty boring. Everyone pretty much just went to bed. Angie and Rose had to sleep on the floor, which neither of them minded. They stayed up late, just lying there and talking.

The next day was pretty dull as well. The graduation wasn't until that night and the party wasn't until Saturday. So they pretty much sat around all day. Rose and Angie played cards and watched TV.

They were watching the Yankees game when Mr. Thompson came in. "Hey aren't they playing in Detroit?" he asked excitedly.

"Um, I think so," Angie said.

"I wonder if your uncle could get us tickets to tomorrow's game."

"Do you think he could?" Angie asked

overjoyed. She had never been to a major league game before.

"I don't know but I'm sure going to ask."

Later that night Mr. Thompson handed Angie an envelope that had "Chief" written on the front. Angie looked from the envelope to her father.

"Why are you giving this to me? What is it?" Angie asked her father, confused.

"Open it up and find out," her father urged with a big grin.

Angie turned the envelope over and tore it open. She pulled out five things that looked like tickets. What were they? Angie still had no idea. Then she turned them over and read: Detroit Tigers vs. New York Yankees. Angie couldn't believe her eyes. Was this a joke? She turned to show Rose but she had already seen the tickets because she stood there staring with her mouth hanging open.

"Are you serious? Are we really going to a Yankees game?" Angie asked, hopeful it wasn't a joke.

"You're holding the tickets aren't you?" her

father said.

It was too good to be true. The two girls couldn't believe it. They were so excited they couldn't sleep that night. They got yelled at, at least five times.

The next day they couldn't wait to go and kept asking how long until they leave. Finally around six o'clock they left for Tiger Stadium. The girls were quiet the whole way there, which was surprising. They found a parking space and headed for the stadium. Once they were inside, the two girls absorbed everything. Their seats were on the first baseline, just behind the bullpen. Angie, Rose and Mr. Thompson went up to the upper deck to have a look around. It was amazing. The view was great. After that the three of them went down to the field to get a closer look. Right in front of them was Andy Pettitte and Joe Girardi warming up. Next to them were Joe Torre and Mel Stottlemyre talking about the game. Mr. Thompson was taking pictures when he pointed to the field.

"Look there's Derek Jeter," he said

"Who's he?" Angie asked looking over at

him.

"He's their new shortstop. This is his first year. He's supposed to be very good," he told the two girls.

Just then as Derek Jeter was heading back to the dugout he stopped a few feet away and started signing books, cards and balls.

"Here, go get his autograph!" Mr. Thompson handed the girls the program.

The two girls walked over nervously. They had opened the book and found a place for him to sign it, right on the scorecard. When he came to them they handed the book to him and he signed it. From that moment on he was the girl's favorite player. After they got the autograph they went to their seats to watch the game.

It was a very exciting game in which the Yankees won. After the game there were fireworks, so they stayed to watch them and then headed home. The two girls didn't stop talking the whole way. They just kept talking about Derek Jeter and how great and hot he was.

The next day when anyone asked the girls

how the game was they were flooded with a play by play of the game. No one could get the girls to talk about anything else but the game.

On Sunday they headed for home. On the way they stopped at Niagara Falls. The girls loved it. They were actually quiet for a whole hour. The rest of the Thompsons cherished the silence.

Chapter Five

It was the best four days of my life, up to that point anyway. I had so much fun. I was so glad I got to share it with you. To this day Derek Jeter is still my favorite player and the hottest one too. I know everything about him.

Junior high was good but not as good as high school. Those were truly the best years of my life, along with the worst. With you as my best friend my life was far from uneventful. So much happened in those four years. Where can I begin? How about when we got our schedules. I couldn't

even read it. And you weren't in my lunch.
I was devastated. What if no one was in
my lunch? Then what was I going to do?
But it all worked out like it always did.
Everyone had been telling us how the high
school was and that we were going to get
lost, but neither of us did. The first month
was a breeze.

We had such fun. We went to
parties, football games, other sporting
events, dances and just about anything else
that was going on. Do you remember the
first dance we went to? I do. We thought
it was going to be so much fun but it turned
out to be kind of a drag.

"Hey do you want to go to the homecoming dance?" Rose asked Angie.

"Yeah! It'll be so much fun! We can get ready at my house and one of my parents can take us," Angie answered all in one breath.

The two girls had decided to go to the dance about a week before. They had a lot to do. They would have to go shopping and find dresses, figure out what to do with their hair and other important things like that. The night of the dance came overnight, it seemed.

"It's about time you got here! Where have you been?" Angie demanded.

"Every time I got to the car I realized I had forgotten something else that I needed to bring. I went back into the house at least ten times."

"Whatever. Come on, we have a lot to do!" Angie said.

The girls got ready in a hurry but still looked amazing. The girls took pictures and then were off to the dance.

The dance was boring but the after party was a blast. Do you remember? Jen asked us to go cuz it was right by her house and she told us we could just stay at her place. That is where I met Jeremy, the love of my life. We started going out about two weeks later. He will always be the love of my life. And he turned out to be my second best friend. And to everyone's surprise my father liked him immediately.

"Rose who is that guy over there? Do you know him?" Angie asked pointing to some guy.

"Um... which one?" Rose asked trying to see which one Angie was pointing too.

"The one talking with the two girls. He's got the blonde spiked hair. He's wearing jeans and a blue shirt."

"Oh him!!! He's really, really cute!!!"

"I know he's the hottest guy I've ever seen!!!!! Do you know him?"

"He's got blue eyes too and an accent I think from down south."

"I've never seen him before."

"I think he's new. They just moved here over the summer, just before school started. But I can't remember where he's from."

"Rose you're killing me!!! Do you know him or not?"

"Oh, I know him. He's in my History and Math classes. All the girls want him."

"Rose are you going to give me a name or will it be faster if I just go and talk to him myself?"

"It might be faster if you go but I know you won't cuz you're too chicken shit to do it."

"That's not true! I'll go and talk to him."

"Yeah right," Rose said, "but you can prove me wrong cuz here he comes."

"Hey Rose," he said with a smile that lit up the room and made Angie go weak in the knees.

"Hi Jeremy. How are you?" Rose asked ignoring the little pull on her sleeve by Angie. "Were you at the dance?"

"Yeah I was there."

"Wish I had known or seen you. I would have liked a dance."

"Yeah well you would have had to wait in line. It seems like everyone wanted to dance with me."

At this Angie couldn't take it anymore and pinched Rose hard on the arm.

"Ouch, that hurt," Rose complained with a smile. "Okay, Okay. Jeremy I'd like you to meet my best friend Angie. Angie this is Jeremy."

"Hi," Angie said extending her hand.

"Hi," Jeremy said taking it. "I have to say that I've been watching you all night and you're the most beautiful girl I've ever seen!!"

"Thank you!" Angie said blushing.

"Can I get you a drink?"

"Sure."

Right from that moment you could tell they would be together forever. They just clicked as if they were always meant to be. Rose was a little jealous that Angie had found someone and she hadn't and that she would now be spending less time with her best friend, but she was still happy for her. They all did everything together. Angie never left Rose out and Rose and Jeremy were like brother and sister.

Chapter Six

"Rose, are you awake?" A voice broke into her thoughts.

Rose couldn't figure out who it was. Then she looked at her clock. It was ten thirty in the morning. She must have fallen asleep while she was reading and reminiscing.

"Rose?" came her mother's voice again.

"Yes Mom, I'm awake," Rose answered groggily. "I fell asleep reading Angle's letter."

"Jeremy's here, dear."

"Okay I'll be down in a minute." Rose rushed to get dressed and go see Jeremy. She needed him now more then anyone.

Jeremy sat in the front room waiting for Rose. He wondered if she was going through the same thing he was. Wondering if Angie had written her a letter too. Jeremy heard something, stood up and turned only to find Rose in his arms. They both breathed a sigh of relief and just held each other. Looking at them you would think that they were boyfriend and girlfriend rather than just friends. They were almost as close as Rose and Angie were. They had spent a lot of time together. After all Jeremy was Angie's fiancé.

"How ya doing?" Jeremy asked letting her go.

"I'm alright, I guess. You?" Rose asked going to sit down.

"I've been better," Jeremy said looking nervous. "Um… did Angie write you a letter too?"

"Yes talking about all the things we've done together. I fell asleep reading it last night. It's like ten pages long. I just finished the part where you two met."

"Yeah mine too. It's killing me. I can barely get through it."

"I know me too."

"Have you thought about what you're going to say tomorrow?"

"Yes, but nothing is coming to me. I feel awful because I should be able to say tons of stuff, but I can't think of one thing."

"That's because you don't want to; you

don't want her to be gone like everyone else."

"What did she say in your letter?" Rose wondered, changing the subject back.

"Just about how we met and everything we've been through and how much she loves me," he said close to tears.

"Oh."

"The Thompsons have been asking about you. They're so worried about you. You haven't been over there since… she passed. They knew you'd take it hard. You spent every waking moment that you could for the past two months with Angie."

"Yeah, well, I guess I just wasn't expecting it to come so soon. I mean I knew it was coming but…" Rose was crying once again.

"It's okay Rose, just let it all out." He held her until she stopped crying. "You're going to the calling hours tonight, right?"

"Yes, of course I am," Rose said shocked.

"Good. I'll be back at six to pick you up; the family is having an hour of privacy."

"Okay, I'll be ready," Rose said. She let

Jeremy out and returned to her room to try and finish the letter.

Chapter Seven

Sophomore year was nothing special. There were the usual sporting events, dances and of course parties. Us getting our licenses. You of course, being an only child and a spoiled brat (lol) got a car so you drove everywhere. Oh yeah how could I forget? There was that one party where you and Tony finally got together.

"Wear something cute," Angie said sitting on Rose's bed helping her get ready for the big party.

"Why?"

"Cuz Jeremy wants you to meet someone," Angie said with a big grin. "He's really cute. I think you'll really like him and who knows maybe you two will hook up."

"Okay but who is it?" Rose asked with a skeptical look on her face.

"I'm not telling," Angie said with a smile. "Are you ready yet? I know it's fashionable to be late but I do want to get there before the party is over."

"HAHA!!! Come on I'm ready," Rose said coming out of the bathroom. "How do I look?"

"Wow. You look great. I love that shirt. I think I have one just like it. Where did you get it?"

"I thought you would like it. I got it from your closet," Rose said with a smile looking down at her shirt.

"Mom, Dad we're going. We'll be back later," Rose called to her parents as they came down the stairs.

"Wait come here," came her father's voice. "Where are you going and what time are you coming home?"

"To the party I told you about earlier."

"Oh yeah, so what time will you be home?"

"Um… two?"

"Um… how about twelve thirty?"

"One thirty please Dad?"

"No, one o'clock!"

"But dad…"

"We'll be home at one Mr. Smith," Angie interjected. "Good night," she finished pulling Rose out the door.

"I could have got one thirty," Rose complained to Angie. "Why did you do that?"

"So we could go. I don't want to get there too late cuz then T…. I mean everyone might be gone."

"Who might be gone?"

"You'll see."

"Will you just tell me? Please?"

"Nope, you can wait five more minutes."

They arrived at the party about ten minutes later. Rose was so nervous. She couldn't wait to see who it was that Angie had picked out for her.

"Let's get something to drink," Angie said leading Rose into the house.

"Wow Rose you look great!!" said their

friend Jen.

"Yeah Rose, who are you looking good for?" asked Kevin, another friend.

"You of course." Rose winked.

"Then will you go out with me tomorrow?"

"Sorry, but I don't think you could handle me." Rose laughed.

"Is that what you think?"

"Yup."

They walked into the kitchen to get some drinks where they stood around and talked to many of their friends. Angie had a Smirnoff and Rose had water seeing as she was the DD.

"Okay, can you tell me now?" Rose asked looking extremely nervous.

"Well you don't have to wait much longer. Here they come now."

"OH MY GOD!!" Rose exclaimed. "That's Tony Cardinal!!! I've had a crush on him forever, ever since freshman year when we had almost every class together. I didn't know Jeremy knew him."

"Yup!! They live by each other. Tony was

the first friend Jeremy made when he moved here. Oh, and you might want to put your tongue back in your mouth before they get here," Angie kidded.

"Hey guys," Jeremy said giving Angie a kiss.

"Hi, Rose," Tony said.

"Oh, you two already know each other?" Jeremy said with a sly grin.

"Yes, which you already knew," Rose replied. "Hi Tony, how have you been?"

"Not bad. I miss having you in all my classes."

"Yeah I know, classes are really boring without you in them."

The four of them joined the party but got bored really fast. So they decided to go out and get something to eat seeing as it was only eleven thirty. They went to Denny's where they ordered breakfast and talked.

"I was so shocked when Jeremy told me he knew you."

"Like I told you before Tony, I don't like to admit I know her; she's a little bit crazy," Jeremy added with a smile.

"Shut up."

"Well, either way I'm glad I found out that he knew you cuz I've wanted to see you again."

"Yeah sure," Rose said.

"No really I did. I've been wanting to talk to you, so I could ask you out," Tony said looking nervous.

"Really, you want to go out with me?" Rose asked unsure.

"Really. I've liked you since freshman year. I was just too chicken shit to ask you out then."

"Well, I've liked you since then too."

The four talked and had a great time. They all got along so well, it was as if they had all known each other since they were born instead of just for a couple of months or years. As they were leaving Tony went to talk to Rose while Jeremy and Angie said goodbye

"So then do you want to go out tomorrow night? Maybe to the movies?"

"Yeah that sounds good. Here, let me give you my number," Rose said trying to hide her excitement.

"Great, I'll give you a call tomorrow."

"K, goodnight."

"Night."

"Goodnight Rose, sleep good honey," Jeremy teased

"Goodnight Jerry-poo," Rose teased right back

"Thank you so much Angie," Rose said on the way home

"For what? It was all you two. You just needed a little push."

Tony asked you out that night and you were so happy. It was great cause now we could double date and if I wanted to spend time alone with Jeremy I didn't have to worry about leaving you anymore.

But junior year was one of the best and one of the worst years of my life.

That year we went to all sporting events, dances and parties. The prom was the best. I went, of course, with Jeremy and you went with Tony. Do you remember? We had such a fantastic time. You won prom queen and Tony won king. It was the happiest I had ever seen you.

Chapter Eight

Then I got really sick. We were worried I would miss finals I was so sick. Luckily I got better enough to take my tests. But then I got really sick again the first week of vacation. I kept getting fevers, chills and I had bruises all over my body that I couldn't explain. So my mom thought maybe we should get it checked out.

You came with me and were there through it all. That meant so much to me seeing as I was so scared. The doctor started with a routine exam and a blood test. Then what came next I don't think any of *us were ready for.*

"Angie I want you to have a bone marrow biopsy and a spinal tap," Dr. Anderson said.

"Why? What's wrong?" Mrs. Thompson inquired looking nervous.

"Well I have an idea but I would rather wait and tell you when I have all the facts. Now I have made some calls and you can have the bone marrow biopsy done tomorrow along with the spinal tap. That way we can get it all done at once. Then I want you to come back the day after and I will have the results for you."

"Doctor I would really like to know why she needs all this," Mrs. Thompson demanded.

"Let's just say, for right now I'm doing it to be safe and I ask that you trust me. I don't want to worry you if there's no reason to."

"Doctor," Angie asked shyly, "can I have Rose in the operating room with me?"

"No I'm sorry she can't, but she is more than welcome to walk you to the door and wait there if you like."

"Okay."

You went with me the next day, walked me to surgery and waited right there till I came out. That meant so much to me. And you were there with me on the worst day of my life giving me strength and encouragement.

"Angie Thompson, the doctor will see you now," the receptionist called.

"Hello, come in and sit down please," the doctor said with a distressed look on his face. "I'm afraid all my fears have been confirmed. Angie, I'm sorry but you have Acute Myeloid Leukemia."

"I have cancer? How? Why?" Angie asked in bewilderment.

"Are you sure?" Mrs. Thompson asked.

"The spinal tap showed fluid in and around the brain and spinal cord. Now we can treat this with chemotherapy. And this may put it into remission."

"And if we decide not to or if the chemo doesn't work, how long will she have?" Mr. Thompson asked so low he could barely be heard.

"Four to six months without, a year or more if chemo doesn't work but stops it a little. But if it does work she will have 40 or more years."

"We want a second opinion," Mr. Thompson said.

"I thought you might, and in the hopes that I was wrong, I sent the test results to some of my colleagues who specialize in this, and they all agree that Angie has Leukemia."

"We need to talk it over first. We'll let you know," Mrs. Thompson said getting up.

"Yes of course. But try and get back to me as soon as possible. You don't want to wait to start treatment."

Chapter Nine

We left the office feeling worse than ever. You had driven and asked me to ride with you. So of course I did and you gave me the most encouraging talk.

"Angie you're my best friend. I can't believe this is happening, it's like a nightmare."

"I know."

"We're going to fight this. I won't let you die. We can get through this. We have too."

"Rose, I don't think there is any way of getting through it," Angie replied in tears.

"Yes there is! We can do this. You have to do chemo. Think of all the things you still have to do, your hopes and dreams. Don't you at least want to try and make them come true?" Rose questioned fighting back tears.

"Yes, but I don't and can't do this alone."

"You don't have to. I'll be by your side every step of the way and so will Jeremy and your family. We're all in this together. Don't ever think you're alone cuz you not!"

You were right, we were in it together. You and Jeremy stuck by me till the end. It was hard but you were there for me no matter what.

After I talked with my parents and told them what I wanted to do, we decided to do the chemotherapy. And the doctor told us that the best one would be intrathecal chemotherapy. I was so scared because they were going to inject it right into the cerebrospinal fluid by going under my scalp.

They said this way it wouldn't hurt as much. It was decided that I would do three chemo treatments. Each treatment for two weeks with a week of recovery in between.

About a week after that horrible day Jeremy took me out to dinner. I couldn't figure out what he was up to. And I got the surprise of my life at the end of dinner. You were the first one we told, remember?

"Rose where are you?"

"At home waiting for Tony, why?"

"Good don't leave; Jeremy and I are on our way over so wait for us."

"Okay." Rose hung up the phone very nervous and a little scared. What if something was really wrong?

Ten minutes later the doorbell rang and

Rose opened the door to see, to her relief the two of them glowing with ear-to-ear grins.

"Rose we want you to be the first to know." Angie smiled.

"Okay what?"

"We're engaged!" Angie answered showing off her rock.

"What! When?" Rose asked giving both of them a hug. "Congrats!"

"Tonight at dinner," Jeremy answered.

"So when's the big day?"

"Well Jeremy wanted to do it over the summer but I think that's a bit soon, after all we're only 17 and we have our whole lives together," Angie informed her.

"That's great! I'm so happy for you!" Rose said giving Angie another hug.

"Thanks! Just one more thing before we go tell the world."

"Yes?" Rose asked.

"Will you be my Maid-of-Honor?" Angie questioned.

"Yes of course," Rose answered with tears

of joy.

I know you were a little sad as you thought you were going to lose me. But you never could. Nothing could ever come between us, not even the love of my life.

As you had promised me you were there every step of the way. You came to all my doctor appointments and went to all my chemo treatments with me. You gave up so much for me and that means the world to me. I know how hard it was for you to break up with Tony. But I know that you felt cause you were always busy with me, that you didn't think it was fair to him. I feel he was the love of your live and I hope that one day you two will be together again.

Chapter Ten

I'll never forget when my hair started to fall out. I thought it was the end of the world. The loss of my hair came with my last set of chemo treatments, two weeks before school would start.

I was horrified. I wasn't going to go to school with half my hair gone. So my parents said that I should just shave the rest of it off. Never in a million years would I do that. But then you convinced me to do it. And how you did it I'll never forget!

"Angie it's me. Do you think you could come over for a little while? I have something I want to talk to you about," Rose asked Angie over the phone.

"I'm not shaving my head, and that's that!" Angie said with a tone of finality in her voice.

"I know, I know and who said anything about shaving your head? I just want to talk about the first day of school. We can look over our schedules."

"I'm not going to school either."

"Fine, will you just come over already? I have something to show you."

"Fine, I'll be over in a few minutes."

When I got there I got the shock of my life. Jeremy met me in the upstairs hallway outside the bathroom, with his head...

"SHAVED!!!!! You shaved you head! Why?" Angie asked almost in tears. She had loved Jeremy's hair.

"I'll tell you in a minute. Rose has something to tell you." Jeremy slowly opened the bathroom door to reveal Rose.

"NO!!!!" Angie cried, tears now rolling down her cheeks. "Why did you do it? Why did you shave your head?"

"So that you would shave yours and not feel self-conscious about it."

"But your hair! Your beautiful curly hair."

"Will grow back, just like yours."

"You can't go to school like that."

"Yes I can. I'll get a wig and so can you."

Angie was crying very hard now. She was so touched that she didn't know what to say, but knew she couldn't refuse.

"Okay," Angie choked out.

"Good, come on we have a lot to do today! Bye Jeremy, we'll see you later," Rose said pulling Angie down the stairs. "We'll go get your head shaved and then we can go get some wigs."

So we went and got my head shaved.
It was hard for me but you were there yet
again.

Chapter Eleven

The day before school I had to go back to the doctor to see if the chemo had worked at all. I was so terrified. What if it hadn't worked? But once again you came with me.

"Angie it's good to see you. You look well. How are you feeling?" Dr. Anderson asked leading them into his office.

"Thank you, I'm feeling pretty good," Angie answered with a smile.

"Well I've look at your test results that we took at the last chemo treatment and it looks as if we got it. There are no fluids or masses anywhere. Congratulations, you are officially in remission."

"Really??" Angie and Rose said together.

The two had never been happier.

Angie called her mom at work and then her dad to tell them the good news. She had insisted that only her and Rose go to the doctor's appointment.

"Where should we go to celebrate?" Rose asked pulling out of the parking garage.

"Let's go get Jeremy and then on to Denny's. I want a sundae," Angie said with a huge smile.

When I got home most of my family was there and your parents too. We had a huge party to celebrate my being as good as new. It was the best day for me.

But the next day was school. I'll never forget going back to school! Our wigs hadn't come in yet and I was going to have to go without it. Well I wasn't going to

go, not without my wig!

"Angie are you up? Rose will be here any minute," came Mrs. Thompson's voice.

"I'm not going!" Angie yelled down to her mom. "They're all going to laugh at me because my head is shaved. I'm not going till I get my wig."

"Rose's head is shaved too and she doesn't have a wig either but she's still going. It isn't fair to make her go if you're not. And what about Jeremy? He shaved his head for you too. After all, they did it for you. No one will make fun of you or say anything."

"Yes they will. Just tell Rose that I don't feel good and I'm sorry."

"No, you can tell her yourself. She's here now."

"Rose, hi! How're you this morning?"

"I'm great. How're you?"

"Well, I don't think I'm going to school today."

"Why, are you sick?"

"No she's not she just doesn't want to go without the wig."

"Thanks Mom."

"Why, Jeremy and I will both be there for you!"

"I know but you aren't in any of my classes and he's only in two with me and it's okay for him to have a shaved head, he's a guy."

"Yeah so? If anyone says anything to you, I'll beat them up! Now come on or we'll be late for our first day of senior year."

"Um… OK!"

"Bye girls, have a good day."

"Bye Mom," the girls said together.

That day was so hard for me. But you met me after every class to make sure that I was okay. That meant a lot to me. There is something about that day, though, that I never told you. I was walking down the hall by myself feeling very self-conscious, when someone stopped me (I can't remember who it was now) and asked me how I was doing and told me that they wished they had a friend like you, someone who would shave their head for them. I continued down the hall and had about three or four more people say the same thing. After the fourth person, I just started crying it meant so much to me, because right then and there I realized how lucky I am to have you as my best friend and that I was glad you made me go to school. There's something else I never told you.

About a week into school Tony came

up to me during lunch. He told me that he was sorry for everything that had happened and everything that was happening. He told me how much he missed you and still loved you and that he understood that you needed to be with me. But that he wished you hadn't broken up with him. He still loved you and he would be there for you and he'd wait for you. I regret now waiting to tell you. I should have told you before prom. Then maybe the two of you could have been back together for it. Even still I'm glad you went together. It was the best night of my life.

Chapter Twelve

"Rose, dinner's ready," Rose heard her mother call.

"Why?" Rose asked out loud as she sat down at the table.

"Why what?" Her father asked.

"Why did it have to come back? She was doing so well until May, until prom," Rose said beginning to cry.

"The doctor told you that even if she went into remission there was always the chance it would or could come back," Rose's mom said soothingly.

"Yes, I know, but she was fine after the treatments. Why did it have to come back?"

"Oh honey," Rose's mom said.

"Do you know what she said to me like a week into school? She told me that what she wanted was to go to prom, be prom queen and graduate high school, like she knew what was going to happen, like she knew she was going to die."

"What?" said Rose's parents together.

"Yeah. So I went and talked with every senior homeroom and told them what she told me. I asked them if they would do it for Angie and all of them said that they had wanted to do it in the first place. So we decided to do it as a surprise. Everyone wrote her and Jeremy's names down. That way they could be king and queen and have it together. And I also convinced them to dedicate the prom to her." Rose was crying so much now it was hard to understand her.

Rose's parents didn't know what to say. She had never told them this. In fact, she had never told anyone this, not Angie, not Jeremy, not even Tony though he knew. She let everyone think it was the senior class's idea and that she just went along with it.

"Where are you going? Rose's mother asked. "You haven't eaten anything."

"I'm not hungry. Jeremy is going to be here in an hour to pick me up. I have to get ready."

Rose went up to her room to get ready but didn't get very far. When she walked into the room the first thing she saw was her prom pictures. At the sight of them all the memories of that wonderful and yet horrible night came flooding back to her.

"Your hair looks so great and I love that dress on you!" Angie and Rose had said at the same time.

"I'm so glad that you're going to prom with Tony!" Angie had told Rose.

"Me too. I still love him and miss him so much."

"Why don't you just tell him?"

"I can't."

"But you love him and he loves you."

"No he doesn't, not anymore, not after all this time."

The guys looked great. There were you and Tony, Jeremy and me, Abby and Nick, Jen and Dave, Erika and Tom, Matt and Ashley, you know the gang. We took about a hundred pictures at Hoopes Park. We ended up with a hummer limo because the company sent us the wrong limo which was okay with all of us. We had the best limo. We went to Abigail's for dinner. It was so nice. Then it was off to the prom at Emerson Park. When we got there you insisted that we go walk on the new pier. I should have known you had something up your sleeve. It was really nice.

"Okay everyone, she will be coming in any minute," Rose informed her senior class.

The pavilion was decorated with Angie's favorite colors: blue and purple. A banner behind the DJ read: "This prom is dedicated to Angie who has touched so many of our lives. You'll never be forgotten. Good Luck. Your senior class." And everyone who was there signed it. Now Angie and Jeremy could be seen coming up the walkway.

The DJ put on one of Angie's favorite songs: "Time of My Life."

"SURPRISE!!" bellowed the class.

Angie stood there paralyzed, not knowing what to say or what to do. She was so overwhelmed. She walked up onto the stage and stared at everyone looking up at her, with tears in her eyes.

"I don't know what to say. This is so wonderful. Thank you. That's all I can say." She cried. "Now this is a party so let's dance the night away."

And that's just what they did. Angie danced with just about everyone who was there. She danced and danced.

"It's time to find out who your king and queen are for your 2002 senior prom."

"Your 2002 Prom King by a unanimous vote is Jeremy Smith."

"OH MY GOD!!!!! Jeremy you won," Angie

squealed as Jeremy stood there perplexed. "Go, go." Angie pushed.

"And now your 2002 Prom Queen by unanimous vote is Angie Thompson!"

"NO!! OH MY GOD!!!! How did you pull this off?"

"Pull what off? asked Rose. "Everyone voted just like me so they did it all on their own. I had nothing to do with it. But I can tell you this, there has never been a more beautiful or deserving Prom Queen then you! I love you Angie!" Rose hugged her best friend.

"I love you too!"

Rose watched as her best friend was crowned queen and in the back of her mind she kept wondering how much longer she had with her. Rose had never seen her friend so happy.

Angie and Jeremy danced their dance to their song, "I Knew I Loved You," by Savage Garden. Angie cried the whole time but loved every minute of it.

"This was really great what, what you did for her," Tony said coming over and putting his arm around Rose.

"She would have done the same for me," Rose said looking up into Tony's eyes. Just when they were about to kiss she looked away, back to where Angie and Jeremy were dancing.

"What's wrong with Angie?" Rose saw that she was kind of leaning on Jeremy as if she couldn't hold herself up. Rose started to go to them but Jeremy held up his hand for her to wait.

After their dance Angie had to sit down. Rose came over and a wave of fear swept through her. Angie was as white as a ghost and looked as if she was going to pass out.

"Come on I'm taking you home now!!" Rose demanded.

"No! I'm fine. I just need to sit for a while," Angie said with difficulty.

"Angie..."

"Rose, this is my prom and I'm not leaving until it's over. You know how much this means to me."

"Okay, if you swear you're okay, we'll stay but no more dancing for a while."

"Deal."

Angie sat for the rest of the dance but did dance the last dance of the night. There was supposed to be a big party after the prom but they decided to get Angie home instead. When they got there Angie's parents were still up. Angie was so tired that she went right upstairs to bed. Mrs. Thompson came running up knowing that something was wrong, with their being home so early.

"What happened? What's wrong?" she demanded.

"Nothing Mom. Just too much dancing." And with that Angie was asleep.

Chapter Thirteen

I paid for all that dancing. I didn't go to school for the whole next week, because I was so weak. But I had the best time and still can't figure out how you pulled off the senior class voting for me to be queen. It was great though. I got a huge welcome back when I did go back to school. Everyone said they were so glad to see me. But that was the week I went back to the doctor for my follow up testing and checkup.

"I'm afraid I have a bit of disheartening

news," the doctor said to the family sitting in front of him. "Angie, your cancer has come out of remission and is spreading... fast."

"What? How can this be? She was doing fine!!!" Mrs. Thompson yelled.

"Angie besides the night at prom have you been feeling unusually tired?"

"Um... yes I have been."

"Well that is a result of your cancer and the fact that it's spreading."

"Can't we do more chemo or try something else?" Mrs. Thompson asked.

"We could but I'm afraid it's spreading too fast and these treatments would have to be doubled if it were to help. And there's still the chance it won't help."

"I don't want to do treatments anymore. I'm done with them," Angie said in final tone of voice.

"How... how long does she have doc?" Mr. Thompson barely breathed.

"August, maybe sooner, maybe longer. There's no way of telling for sure."

"What?" Rose shrieked out loud.

Everyone was so upset that day. But I really wasn't. I guess it just hadn't really hit me yet that I was really going to die. I still don't think it has. But everything worked out. I finished high school and graduated with honors. Everyone stood and clapped for me when I got my diploma. It was wonderful. I cried, of course. Our graduation parties were together and everyone was there. It was a great day. And now we had the challenge of making this the best summer of our lives.

Chapter Fourteen

"Rose, Jeremy is here."

"Okay Mom, I'll be right down."

"Hi! Are you ready?"

"Yeah."

"Bye honey, we'll see you there."

"Okay Mom."

They drove there in silence, not wanting to say anything. Not wanting to be going to where they were bound. They pulled into the funeral home only to see Steve and Dan outside staring into space. Rose got out of the car and walked over to them.

"How are you guys holding up?" she asked giving them both a hug.

"Not good sis," Steve said not letting her go. "You were always such a good friend to her. Thank you."

At this Rose started to cry. This was her second family and she hated seeing them like this. It wasn't fair.

They all walked in together. When they got there Tony was standing there waiting.

"Tony," Rose said going over and giving him a hug. "I'm so glad you're here."

"So am I, so am I."

As they walked down the aisle toward the casket they saw that it was lined with pictures, ones of Angie when she was a baby and a little girl, ones from school, prom, parties and sporting events. Most of them had Rose in them too. As she looked at them she saw one that made her cry on the spot. It was the one of her, Jeremy and Angie, just after they all got their heads shaved and had huge smiles on their faces.

As they turned and started to walk toward the casket, Rose turned to run out of the room, but Tony caught her.

"I can't do this," she said, tears streaming down her face. "I can't say goodbye to her."

"Yes you can and you have to. Do it now before everyone gets here. I'm right here beside you. We'll do it together."

They walked up to the casket hand in hand.

At the sight of her best friend looking so white and waxy, Rose lost it. She stayed at the side of the casket for a long time just looking at Angie. Angie had the best friend necklace that they had bought when they were ten. The engagement ring Jeremy gave her was on her finger and she was holding red roses, her favorite. She looked so peaceful, so beautiful.

When Rose finally got up she went over to Mr. and Mrs. Thompson.

"How are you holding up dear?" Mrs. Thompson asked giving her a hug and fighting back tears.

"Not so good. I just miss her so much," Rose said crying again.

"I know we all do," Mrs. Thompson said, tears streaming down her cheeks and soaking her neatly pressed silk shirt.

Slowly people started to trickle in to pay their respects. It seemed as if all of Auburn was there. They just kept coming. And as Rose looked around and saw all these people, many that she knew and many that she didn't, she realized how big a heart her best friend really had. Calling hours were from five to eight but because there was such an outpouring of affection, they didn't stop until almost ten thirty.

Everyone who came stayed for at least half an hour or more. It was as if they didn't want to go because if they left then it would really be true, she would really be gone.

Tony gave Rose a ride home. It was pretty quiet most of the way home.

"Rose?" Tony broke the silence.

"Yes?"

"I love you and I just want you to know that I'm here for you no matter what you're going through. You can always come to me," Tony told her.

"Thank you, you have no idea how much that means to me," Rose said opening the door and getting out. "And Tony, I love you too," she said closing the door and heading to the house.

Chapter Fifteen

Rose was exhausted when she got home. But she just couldn't sleep. What would she say tomorrow? Instead of going to bed she pulled out Angie's letter and decided to finish it.

We wanted to go on a road trip but my parents wouldn't let me. They were too worried and also wanted to spend time with me. It was the best summer. We went out to Jeremy's camp every weekend and had a big campfire and party. And during the week we hung out with friends and with my family. It's been too short of a time. I want more time with everyone. I'm going to miss you so much!

But I want you to know that I'm not afraid. I'm not scared to die anymore. I've learned to accept it and I think you should too. I'll be all right and so will you. I'm ready whenever God wants me. I'm ready. Just know that I'll always be with you in everything you do and everywhere you go. I love you and I'll miss you. You'll always be by best friend. I LOVE YOU SO MUCH!!! I'll be waiting for you, at the gates of HEAVEN.

Your Best Friend Forever,

Angie XXX 7/20/02

Rose was in tears after reading the ending. And after looking at the date she realized that Angie had finished this letter only the day before she died. She couldn't believe it. Rose remembered how hard those last days were for everyone. She was allowed to spend her last days at home instead of at the hospital. Angie was so tired that she slept most of the time. At most she was awake for only about ten minutes at a time. Rose had spent much of her time at the Thompson's house. She slept there and ate there.

It was about four thirty in the afternoon on July 21, 2002. Rose was the only one in the room with Angie. Angie had said her goodbyes to everyone but Rose. Rose was at the bedside when Angie woke up.

"Rose, are you there?" Angie asked in barely a whisper.

"I'm here, I haven't left."

"I'm glad. You know you're my best friend right?"

"Yes of course and you're mine."

"I want you to know that I'll never forget

you and everything you've done for me. I'll always be there for you. So go out there and be the best person you can be. Don't be sad. I'll be fine and so will you. I'm ready to go and I'm not scared. I love you Rose."

And with that Angie was gone. It was as if she had just slipped back off to sleep. Rose sat there at the bedside crying, not knowing what to do. Her best friend was gone forever.

Rose walked out of the room into the hallway where Angie's family was waiting.

"She's gone," Rose wept into Jeremy's arms.

Mrs. Thompson fell into her husband's arms with grief. Mr. Thompson held her with tears streaming down his face. Dan and Steve sat there and stared into space, crying silently not knowing what to do. Rose walked past them and went downstairs to the rest of the family and friends to tell them that Angie was gone. Rose didn't have to say a word though, they all knew just by the look on her face.

That was three days ago, but it seemed like

a lifetime to Rose. She hadn't left her room much since then. But today was the day of the funeral and she still didn't know what to say.

Chapter Sixteen

The whole way to the funeral home she ran ideas through her head but kept coming up with nothing that said what she really felt and who Angie really was. Then when they got to the funeral home, Rose looked at her second family and finally realized what she needed to say. Everyone who she loved in the world was in this small room. And she loved all these people because of one person, her best friend.

They all paid their last respects and headed to church. Rose rode in a car with Jeremy and Tony. Rose knew this was going to be the hardest day of her life but she knew she would make it through with the help of family and friends.

When they got to the church they couldn't believe all the people that were there. There were more people here today then last night. There were so many people they were standing in the back and in the aisles.

The mass was beautiful. Rose was anxious

the whole time. What if she couldn't say anything, what if nothing came out? It was almost time and Rose was very nervous.

She walked slowly up the aisle, stopped briefly at Angie's casket, then walked up to the podium. She looked out into the crowd smiling at people she knew. Then she looked at the Thompsons and all her nerves disappeared.

"Last night I hoped and prayed that when I woke up this morning all this would be a really bad dream and that I'd go down to breakfast and the phone would ring and it would be Angie calling to tell me to hurry up and get my butt over to her house. But it wasn't and I knew that when I went downstairs and my parents were dressed in black. Then I realized that I had to give a speech in two hours and didn't have a thing to say. What could I possible say? I had grown up with Angie. We had done everything together since Kindergarten. We were going to go to the same college and room together and I was going to be maid-of-honor in her wedding. She was my best friend and yet I was mad at her for dying. How could she die? Why didn't she fight harder? It wasn't fair, she ruined all our plans. It was all her fault for getting sick. Then I was mad at myself for letting her die, for breaking my promise to her.

"Then I got to the funeral home and church this morning and realized something. I had been feeling sorry for the wrong things. In fact I should have been helping the Thompsons through it all but I wasn't. Instead I locked myself in my room and refused to leave. Like I thought doing this would bring her back. But it didn't. Then I looked at the Thompsons and realized they weren't crying and although I know they're sad, they don't seem it. And that's when I realized that Angie is in a better place, that she isn't suffering anymore and that she's still here with all of us in our hearts.

"So what kind of person was Angie? Well, look around you, look at all the people here today. This is a show of how big Angie's heart was. She touched every person here in one way or another. Whether it was when she said hi to you when you were having a bad day, or she helped you pick up your books when you dropped them, or she invited you to sit at her lunch table because you were alone or because you were one of her good friends or a complete stranger. She always wanted people to feel that they had a friend in her if no one else. She had a big heart and always wanted to help and was always willing to help no matter what it cost her.

"I know if she was here right now she would want me to thank everyone here for all you did for her no matter how big or small. Whether you said hi in the halls or you helped her with her homework, or you supported her and wished her the best throughout her illness. I also know she would want me to say thank you to all of her classmates who helped to make her senior prom the best night of her life. And it truly was; she didn't stop talking about it for weeks.

"Steve, she hopes you find what you want in your life, and to be the best you can be; just remember how much she loves you. Dan, she also hopes the best for you and wishes you all the best luck in the world with Marie. She's watching over you two and loves you very much. Jeremy, she loved you more than anything and I know that you are sad now and couldn't possibly think of ever loving another, but she just wants you to be happy. Don't waste it loving her memory; find someone else and love her as you loved Angie. That's what she wants. Mr. and Mrs. Thompson, Angie loves you more than you could ever know and even though she didn't always show it, she did and wanted me to tell you. She also wanted me to tell you to let her go, and she's in a better place. She doesn't want you to stop living because she's gone. Cherish her memory by the happy times not the sad ones. Don't be sad but glad that she touched so many lives and that you raised a young woman who everyone loved. She was ready to go and had no regrets about leaving. She's in a better place looking down on us all and wishing us the best for wherever our paths may take us. She wouldn't want us to be sad at her death but to celebrate her life. So I say let's do that for Angie. Let's not be sad that she is gone but happy that we were lucky enough to have known her." Rose ended with tears in her eyes.

Looking out over the church she could see everyone was crying but knew that this would be the end of their tears and they would later celebrate Angie's life.

When she went to take her seat, Mr. and Mrs. Thompson, Dan and Steve all gave her a hug and thanked her for everything. Rose only looked at them with tears streaming down her cheeks and gave them a weak smile.

After the mass they headed to the cemetery. It was a bright sunny day. Everyone who was at church went. The priest said his final prayer and everyone said their last goodbyes. Slowly everyone started to leave. The only people who stayed were the Thompsons, Jeremy, Tony and Rose. After about ten minutes the Thompsons left to head back to the house before the crowd came. Jeremy just stood there with tears streaming down his face. Rose turned and gave him a hug. He just cried into her shoulder. After a few minutes he let her go and looked at her.

"She didn't love anyone as much as she loved you, not even me. Don't waste your life on her memory either, she wouldn't want that," Jeremy said, kissing her check and heading for the car to wait for her and Tony.

Rose looked at the casket that now held her best friend and started to cry. Tony put his arm around her and held her.

"It's not fair. This shouldn't have happened to her."

"You're right it shouldn't have, but it did," Tony said trying to comfort her. "But instead of being sad that she's gone, be happy that you got to know her and that she was a part of your life. Take your own advice and be happy."

Rose wiped her tears and smiled. He was right. She would listen to her own advice.

She looked at Tony and smiled. Then she put her arms around him and gave him a hug.

As she did she whispered in his ear, "Thank you, I love you so much." And then she kissed him.

"I love you too. Will you marry me?" he whispered on her lips.

"What?"

"I know it seems like horrible timing but I

couldn't think of a better time. Angie always did want us to be together."

"Yes, I'll marry you," she said kissing him again. "Are you happy now?" she added to Angie's casket, tears of joy now streaming down her cheeks.

"I'll meet you at the car, take your time."

"Thanks," Rose said turning back to the grave.

"Well Angie, I can't believe this is the end, that this is goodbye. We had some really great times, didn't we? No one could ever replace you as my best friend. Don't worry, I'll take good care of Jeremy for you until he finds someone else and I won't let him be alone, I promise. And don't worry, I'll take care too," Rose said touching the casket. "I just can't believe you're gone. What am I going to do without you? Who will I go to with all my problems, worries, hopes and dreams? You know everything and now you're gone. How am I to go on? Angie I love you so much! You'll always be my best friend. Best friends forever!" At this Rose half walked half ran back to the car so she wouldn't lose it again.

They got to the house and parked the car. There were tons of people there. Rose stopped and stared at the house. This had been her second home for so long. She had so many memories at this house. She couldn't imagine walking in and Angie not being here. Rose almost turned and ran up the street to get away from the place that once held her happiest memories. But Tony and Jeremy each grabbed a hand as if they knew what she was thinking and guided her into the house.

Everyone was smiling and having a good time. They were all telling their favorite stories of Angie. Rose just looked around and said to herself, "This is what Angie wanted." Most people only stayed for an hour or so and then left. Only those who were really close to Angie stayed late.

Rose stayed to help clean up so the Thompsons wouldn't have to.

"Rose, I just want to thank you for everything you've done for Angie over the years. You've been such a good friend to her."

"She was a good friend to me as well and

she would have done the same for me."

"Well I was wondering if tomorrow, or maybe in a couple of days, you could come by and go through her stuff with me. I know a lot of her stuff has special meaning to you. You can have her clothes or any anything else. There are only a few things I want to keep," Mrs. Thompson said in a choked voice.

"Of course I will."

"And don't think that just because Angie is gone that you can't still come over here. You're part of this family and are welcome over here any time."

"I know, and don't worry, it would take a restraining order to keep me away. You're my family and nothing will ever change that." At this they hugged and cried into each other's arms.

Rose said her goodbyes and headed home. Her parents were waiting up for her. She walked over to them and gave them both a kiss.

"I love you guys so much!! Thanks for everything you've done for me."

"How're you doing honey?" her father

asked looking concerned.

"I'm fine." She smiled and headed upstairs.

She went to her room and got ready for bed. She got into bed and thought about the day. She really would be okay. She fell asleep with the thought of Angie watching over her, with that big grin on her face.

Epilogue

It had been almost a month since Angie had died but with each passing day it got easier to go on. Rose was now getting ready to go away to school. As she packed her things she thought about Angie. Rose didn't think she would be able to do it. She couldn't go without her best friend; these were their plans and without Angie it just didn't feel right.

The morning had finally arrived for Rose to leave for school. But on this morning Rose was starting to feel uneasy about going. She couldn't leave. But why not? Tony and Jeremy would be there to keep her company and help her through. But something was bothering her.

Then the phone rang pulling her back to life.

"Hello?"

"Hey it's Tony. I'm on my way to Jeremy's, then we'll be over to get you. Are you ready?"

"Yes, I just have to do something before we go. Give me like a half hour okay?"

"Sounds good, see you then. I love you."

"I love you too," Rose said hanging up the phone and heading out the door. "Mom I'll be back. I have to go out for a few minutes." She had to go see Angie before she left.

When she got to Angie's grave she stood there just looking at it for a while.

"So Tony and I are trying to plan the wedding. We're thinking of next summer. I can't wait, I love him so much." Rose rambled avoiding the real reason she was there. "We leave for school today. How can I go without you? We made these plans together. I don't think I can go." Rose was now crying which she hadn't done since the day Angie was buried. And she came here almost every day.

She touched the gravestone and felt a wave of calm come over her. It was as if Angie had just told her to go and that it was alright, that she would be there, that she wasn't leaving her. She was going with her in her thoughts and most of all in her heart.

Rose wiped away her tears. She smiled to

herself, turned and walked into the bright fall morning.

Rose knew that she could go on with her life and that Angie would always be in her heart and thoughts. Rose would live her life for Angie, her best friend forever.

Made in the USA
Charleston, SC
17 May 2011